Lebendiges Englisch 1

The Travellers

Eine Lektüre zum Gebrauch
nach Lektion 15,
Lebendiges Englisch Band 1.

Max Hueber Verlag

Bearbeitungen von James Aller

CIP-Kurztitelaufnahme der Deutschen Bibliothek

> Lebendiges Englisch. – München [i. e. Ismaning]: Hueber
> Teilw. bearb. von Hans G. Hoffmann
> NE: Hoffmann, Hans G. [Bearb.]
> 1.
> Lektüre 1. The travellers : e. Lektüre zum Gebrauch nach
> Lektion 15, Lebendiges Englisch Bd. 1 / [Bearb. von James Aller].
> – 1. Aufl., 1. Dr. – 1983.
> ISBN 3-19-302191-1

1. Auflage

3. 2. 1. | Die letzten Ziffern
1987 86 85 84 83 | bezeichnen Zahl und Jahr des Druckes.
Alle Drucke dieser Auflage können nebeneinander benutzt werden.
© 1983 Orlando Language Texts Ltd, Bath
Gesamtherstellung: Sulzberg-Druck GmbH, Sulzberg im Allgäu
Printed in Germany
ISBN 3-19-302191-1

Inhalt

The Pilot	4
The Little Boy	11
A Taxi Isn't Always Just A Taxi	14
A True Story	16
Too Young	17
When In Rome,	24
A Most Unusual Journey	28
At The Enquiries Desk	29
First Stop Mars	32
Robinson Crusoe's Diary	41
The Final Problem (Sherlock Holmes)	44
Anecdotes (Cecil Torr)	51
Word List	53
Acknowledgements	63

The Pilot

Martin Brennan was a pilot, but he did not know the Far East at all. At work, his flights took him to Europe and America. And because he travelled a lot anyway, he never wanted to travel to other places in his free time. He always spent his holidays in quiet English villages, a long way from planes and airports and check-in desks.

But now, here he was, a long way east and a long way from home. He felt quite different, and really it was quite exciting. It wasn't because Malaka was a tourist resort. Malaka wasn't a tourist resort. It had only one hotel, and that wasn't really for foreigners. It was more for Keran travellers coming from the towns up north, on their way to Changkorn to see government ministers, or businessmen who wanted to sell things in the towns down the coast. No-one stayed there for more than one night, said the man in reception with a shrug. But Brennan didn't mind. Malaka was exciting, and something had to happen. Something always happened in the Far East, his pilot colleagues told him. That was why he was spending his holiday here this year, not in Devon.

Brennan wanted excitement. He looked at the map and his choice fell on Malaka because it had to be exciting. It was small, it was a long way from important places, but it was in a busy, developing country. The country was always in political chaos. Year after year there were plots, and rumours of plots in the newspapers. Then, two years ago, Hamdang Amdjan became president, a strong man. Of course, newspapers in London, New York and Frankfurt talked about plots against Amdjan, too, but he was still there. Recent reports in the newspapers said there were plots against Amdjan in high places. Very high places, some said, and talked of ministers and even prime ministers.

But to Brennan, who was sitting in a café in Malaka with a cup of peppermint tea in front of him, everything seemed normal. Daily life in Malaka was busy, like in all market towns. People went in and out of the bazaar. Dirty old cars, full of young men, pushed between the country people, who carried their goods on their heads. Out of every dark window came popular music from cheap transistor radios or the voices of children who tried to imitate it. Brennan didn't mind the music or the people. It was different, and it was exciting. It was not like Devon at all. No-one looked at him, and he enjoyed that.

But it seemed that someone looked at him after all. On his second evening in Malaka, he was in the little restaurant near the hotel, eating his rice. A shadow fell on his plate. He looked up and saw a man in elegant clothes.

"Do you mind if I sit down?" asked the man in a clear Sandhurst voice, and sat down before Brennan could say anything.

"You are here on holiday, I expect," said the man. "Do you like Malaka?"

"Your English is excellent," said Brennan. He didn't have anything else to say. Of course he liked Malaka. It was exciting. It was different. "Yes, I like Malaka very much." The man laughed.

"But I think you don't know our language very well," he said.

"No," said Brennan. "I'm sorry, I don't know your language at all."

The man laughed again.

"I'm sorry," he said, "I'm not being polite. My name is Samdi. Colonel Samdi."

"I'm Martin Brennan," said Brennan. "I'm a pilot."

Samdi's English was really very good, and for about ten minutes the two men talked about this and that. They talked about the economies of their two countries, about life in market towns, about popular music.

After a time, Samdi seemed to lose interest in the conversation. He did not answer one of Brennan's questions, and the expression on his face became odd. Then he said, "It isn't very nice here. Can we go somewhere else? Do you mind?"

Again, Brennan did not know what to say.

"Why don't you come and stay with me while you're in Malaka?" Samdi went on. "I've got a very big house, and I expect you'll find it comfortable enough."

Brennan looked over the road at the dirty hotel, then said, "All right. That's very kind of you."

Samdi called the hotel boy over to the café, said something to him in a quiet voice, and the boy went back to the hotel. A few minutes later he came back with Brennan's luggage. It was all ready.

The two men got into Samdi's jeep, and the boy put the luggage on the back seat. They moved off between the people who were walking down the street with goods on their heads.

The journey took about 15 minutes. They drove up the hill out of the town, and stopped in front of Samdi's house. It was a small tidy villa with dark green trees around it. A guest room was all ready for Brennan when they got out. This was a surprise to Brennan, but not to anyone else. In fact, no-one in the villa showed surprise at all.

"But then, things are different here," thought Brennan. "It's a different culture."

Only after a few days did Samdi talk about the plane. He was very interested in Brennan's work as a pilot. Did he sometimes fly through bad weather? Did he like night flights? Did he know how to land on short landing strips?

Yes, said Brennan, he knew all the problems, they teach things like that at the pilots' school. All good pilots can do things like that.

Samdi looked very happy. Then he frowned. There was a problem, he explained, perhaps Mr Brennan could help. He (Samdi) worked for the government, and he admired the President. But there were dangers for the President. There were plots against him and his government. People in high places wanted to kill the President. But loyal members of the government had made plans for the safety of the President. They were arranging everything now. The President would travel at night, by special plane from the little airport near Malaka, to a safe place in another country.

Brennan was amazed. He did not even know that there was an airport in Malaka.

"No, it's a special military airport," explained Samdi. Then Brennan saw the same odd expression on his face.

"Perhaps you can help us," said Samdi after a few minutes. "We do not have a good pilot. I mean, a trustworthy pilot. You understand?"

Brennan looked at him. No, he did not understand. "I see I must be very clear," said Samdi. "We need a good pilot. You are a good pilot. Perhaps you can be our trustworthy pilot."

Brennan sat suddenly back in his chair, and did not answer. This was the excitement of Malaka, then. He wanted excitement, and here it was. But, now it was here, did he want it? Excitement was danger, too. Was Samdi trustworthy? What did he really want?

He closed his eyes and thought, Shall I or shan't I?

He opened his eyes.

"Yes," he said. "I'll do it. What do you want?"

Samdi said, "Shhh", and listened for a few minutes. No-one said anything, and they could not hear anything outside. Then, in a quiet, reasonable voice, Samdi started to explain the plans.

"On Monday night at 11 p.m, a plane will land at Malaka airport. Amdjan will arrive from Changkorn by jeep, about 30 minutes later. Your flight to Senala will take about 2 hours. In Senala, a number of loyal officers will be waiting for you. If you like, you can stay in Senala for the rest of your holiday, or you can go home on the next plane. That is your choice. We will arrange that for you, of course."

Samdi's voice seemed suddenly quiet. He explained the details again; but to Brennan it seemed that, suddenly, the room was dark.

"If you don't mind," he said, "I'll go back to my hotel."

"Of course," said Samdi. "We'll get a taxi for you."

The few days until Monday seemed to go very quickly. At ten o'clock in the evening, Samdi and Brennan drove out to the little airport. It was just a landing strip – there were no buildings.

Brennan felt in his pocket the thick roll of banknotes. Samdi gave them to him "in gratitude" after breakfast that morning.

"Our country will always thank you for your help," he said in his quiet voice. Brennan saw that odd expression again.

At five minutes to eleven they heard the engines of a small plane. The plane was obviously in a building among the trees near the landing strip. Why couldn't he see the building? And suddenly, there was the plane behind him. Four men were pulling it out on to the landing strip.

He frowned, and walked over to the plane. Mmm. A Piper. No problems there.

He looked at his watch. Five past eleven. Where was the jeep with Amdjan? He couldn't hear anything, only the noises from the forest.

They sat there in the night for two hours. During this time he only saw Samdi for one minute. He was with the four men around the plane, talking to them quickly. Then he disappeared again for an hour.

An hour later he came back and called Brennan over to them. Something was obviously wrong, he said. The plane could not wait any longer.

"It will be better if you fly the plane with the copilot over to Ana Lanaga now. From there you can take the plane home."

"Odd," thought Brennan. " Where does this copilot come from?" Then he thought, "Why are they coming? Before, it was only me and Amdjan."

Now there were only three people there. Two of the men were obviously no longer with them. Perhaps they were somewhere in the forest. Samdi and the two others went over with him to the plane and got in. They took off and flew into the night.

So Brennan never saw Senala. And, after the experience in Malaka, he didn't want to spend much time in Ana Lanaga. He took the next plane home, back to the safety of England.

For some days he sat in his garden and looked at the flowers. Then he called his friend Mike on the phone.

"Where have you been?" asked Mike.

"Oh, on holiday in Malaka."

"Good God, not there!"

"Why? What's wrong with Malaka? asked Brennan.

"Haven't you heard?" asked Mike with a laugh. "You are naive, old man. There have been reports in the newspapers about a plot to kill Amdjan. Didn't you know?"

"No. It was very quiet in Malaka."

"Yes! Well, it seems that a number of army officers told Amdjan about a plot to kill him. They said he must go to Senala, for his own safety, and arranged for a plane for him. But in fact it was a plot against Amdjan. The officers wanted to shoot down the plane on its way to Senala. I expect they were going to put a bomb on it, or something."

"Good God," said Brennan. His face was white.

"Yes. Well, anyway, it seems Amdjan stayed at home, and the officers had to leave on the plane. I hope there wasn't a bomb on it."

He laughed.

Brennan put down the phone. His hand trembled. He went over to the drinks cupboard and poured out a large glass of whisky. He closed his eyes and drank it.

The Little Boy

It was Easter Monday, and the train was very full. In fact, it was so full that the porter had to push my suitcase through the window from the corridor. So I gave him something extra, also through the window, to thank him for his help. After all, it was he who found me the seat when I thought there weren't any seats at all.

I took out my newspaper and started to read. Then, one minute before the train left, someone pushed open the door to the corridor.

"Can I ask one of you kind gentlemen if you'll look after this little boy on the journey, and tell him when he has to get off? He's getting off at Hove."

We all tried to look like unkind gentlemen. But his mother (if that's who she was) was already pushing the little boy into our compartment between the legs of us various kind (or unkind) gentlemen.

"Be a good boy, Harry, when you get to Hove. And write to me," she said to him, as she closed the door with a bang.

I looked down, and saw a small boy with a dirty face and a large hoop. He grinned back at me. I pushed him over to the window, where there was room for him and his hoop. Just then, the train started to move. Harry's mother waved good-bye to him from the platform. In my pocket, I found some sweets, so I gave one to Harry, to keep him quiet. This was a big mistake. It was now clear to Harry who was the 'kind gentleman' in the compartment. Obviously, it was now my job to look after him for the whole journey.

The hoop swung round in gratitude, and hit me on the head. Then it swung round again and hit the old man in the next seat, just as he was going to tell the boy to be careful. No-one found this funny. The old man held on to the hoop, and tried to push it under the seat. But there was no room for it between the legs and the luggage. So he gave it back to Harry, saying,

"You be careful, my boy."

Harry grinned at him, and dropped the hoop on the old man's right foot.

As the train left Gatwick Airport, a railway official pushed down the corridor, asking for passengers' tickets.

"Tickets, please!" he called.

Everyone in the compartment heard him, but we all waited until he opened the door of the compartment before we looked for our tickets. We showed him our tickets.

"Where's your ticket, son?" said the offical, looking at Harry.

"Don't know," said Harry, and grinned at him.

No-one said anything, so I said,

"I expect it's in his pocket."

This was my second big mistake. We looked in Harry's pockets. There was only a platform ticket in them. The official looked at me, so I paid Harry's fare for him.

The railway official closed the door of the compartment and staggered on down the corridor.

"Perhaps you'll have to pay his return ticket, too," said the old man.

At Balcombe, I offered Harry another sweet. Harry took the sweet, and it fell out of his hand as he was putting it into his mouth. He picked it up and put the dirty sweet into his mouth.

At Burgess Hill, there was a catastrophe. The tall man in the middle suddenly decided that this was his stop and he wanted to get out. Someone told him that this was not possible. This information was probably quite true. There was no room for him to get out. However, the tall man threw his bag out into the corridor through the window, and walked over our feet after it. He wasn't quite successful in this, because his foot was inside Harry's hoop, and he started to take the hoop with him. In fact, he almost fell through the window into the corridor. However, because of all the people in the corridor, this was not possible, and he fell on the hoop. It broke, and Harry started to cry. It was terrible. Even sweets could not stop it. The other passengers in the compartment looked at me, and I could see what they were thinking. It was my fault.

The train started to move. Harry cried all the way from Burgess Hill to Hassocks. At Hassocks, he decided it was time to get out, and he tried to climb through the window. The old man tried to help him through the window, but I told Harry in a stern voice,

"This is not your stop, Harry. And don't cry. We're almost there now. Only another ten minutes."

I pushed another sweet into his mouth, just as the train went into a tunnel. The crying stopped suddenly. I thought it was the sweet. But it wasn't, it was the tunnel. Harry liked the tunnel. It was a new experience.

Suddenly we were in Hove, and we could see the sea. A lot of people got out, and Harry and I did, too. A large woman in a red pullover came up to us as we got off the train. She looked at me.

"You bad boy," she said to Harry. "You know you mustn't talk to strangers."

She took him by the hand, without a word, took his bag out of my hand and marched off. I got back on the train.

Someone was sitting in my seat.

A Taxi Isn't Always Just A Taxi

When the car gets near the border, the car stops. The passenger in the front seat gets out, goes round to the back, takes out the baggage there, and gets into the boot of the car. The driver puts back the baggage and somehow closes the boot, and then the car goes on to the border with its passenger in the boot. After the border, the car stops again, the driver opens the boot and takes out the baggage; the man behind it gets out and climbs back into the passenger seat inside the car. There he stays until the next international border.

It is not a very comfortable way of travel, but it is an easy way to get into a country like Britain without a passport. These days, there are a number of organizations in this modern smuggling business – the smuggling of people. The smugglers are taxi-drivers from the Continent. Most illegal immigrants are Asians, from the countries of the old British Empire like India and Pakistan. And the taxi-drivers have made large profits from their smuggling business, since the introduction of strict control of immigration a few years ago. People wanting to come to Britain are often ready to pay a lot of money, and they are also ready to accept the risks.

Interpol is, of course, trying to find out the people who control the smuggling business. At the borders, police check cars, especially taxis from particular countries. But the smugglers can always find new ways to bring in their cargoes. They often have cars with a double boot. The illegal immigrant has to get into the one under the baggage boot. When the car is travelling over the Continent, he doesn't have to stay there very long. But on the last part of the journey – from the Continent over the sea to Britain – he can sometimes spend up to four or five hours, if he is unlucky. So the illegal immigrant takes off most of his clothes, otherwise it gets too hot inside his little box.

The really bad moment for the taxi-drivers is when they arrive in Britain. The normal form of travel is by boat, arriving in the early morning. This is because, in the early morning, the night immigration officials are getting ready to leave, and their day-time colleagues are just arrving. The night officials are of course tired, and so they will perhaps not look hard for smugglers.

Even so, the immigration police are arresting more and more taxi-drivers. One particular driver was too interested in the money. He put three men into his boot – the boot was not big enough even for one man. His three 'passengers' died, and the police found them. Another driver didn't see the police car following him. He stopped at the arranged place outside London and opened the boot. His 'passenger' got out and fell into the hands of a waiting police officer. Another police officer arrested the taxi-driver who 'helped' the illegal immigrant into the country.

A True Story

An expensive, new Jaguar car is driving along the motorway at high speed. A police car overtakes it, showing its STOP sign, and so the Jaguar stops. A policeman gets out of the police car and walks over to the Jaguar with an important expression on his face.

"Hello, and congratulations, sir. You have just won one hundred pounds! Your car was the first car to drive on this new part of the motorway," says the policeman. The expression on his face becomes almost friendly. "Can I ask you something? What will you do with the money?"

"I think I'll pay for a few driving lessons with it, so that I can take my driving test," answers the man in the Jaguar.

"Don't you listen to him, officer," says the pretty blonde girl in the front passenger seat. "He's drunk and talking nonsense."

Before the officer can say anything, a voice from the back of the car complains, "Didn't I tell you? I knew you couldn't get very far in a stolen car."

Too Young

"You want to do *what* this summer?" said Helen Mitchell in a sharp voice, looking at her daughter.

"We want to hitch-hike through Europe," said Anita, this time taking her hand from in front of her mouth.

"Perhaps down to Greece, if we can," she added. She hoped that her voice sounded casual.

"You can't be serious," said her mother. "At your age!" She turned to her husband.

"George! Are you listening? I've never heard anything like it! George! I'm talking to you!"

"Yes, yes, my dear, I'm listening. I heard Anita the first time." He put down his newspaper on the sofa beside him.

"And just who is *we*, anyway?" Helen went on.

"Rolf Casey, from college. He's doing French and Greek. He's in his second year!"

Anita thought she sounded very cool, not hysterical and silly like her mother.

"Never heard of him! And if he's only a second-year student, he can't be more than 18 or 19. Much too young. It's out of the question, isn't it, George!"

"And if I say he's 30, that's too old for me, I suppose," said Anita. "Anyway, you *do* know him, mother. He's brought me home after concerts or dances lots of times. Last Saturday evening, you even asked him in for coffee. But of course, you don't remember that."

I can be just a little bit bitter, she thought. It's all so silly of mother.

"This whole holiday is his idea, I suppose," said her mother.

Anita tried to sound casual.

"Well, yes, I suppose it was. But I was talking about holidays, and France and Italy, and places like that, and he said, Why don't we go to France and Italy on holiday? I said, we haven't got enough money for the fare even, so he said, Why don't we hitch-hike?"

She stopped, and then added, "I think it's a good idea. What's wrong with it?"

George Mitchell looked up from his newspaper.

"I suppose he's already travelled around Europe a lot," he asked. He didn't sound very interested.

"Well, no, he hasn't, really," said Anita. "But he's been to Scotland with his parents."

It didn't sound very good, even to her. Obviously her mother thought the same.

"So," said her mother, "so that's it, is it? You don't know anything about Europe, he doesn't know anything about it, and the two of you want to go off there, without a penny in your pockets, like a pair of tramps."

She added, "Anyway, he seems a real dreamer to me."

"I thought you didn't know Rolf, mother," said Anita. Her mother didn't listen.

"The trouble is," she went on, "you have too much holiday. Nine weeks is much too long. Why don't you stay at home and study for your exams?"

"Oh, mother, what an idea! The holidays are for fun. Anyway, Rolf has to learn French and Greek. If we go to France and Greece, he can practise. It's good for his work."

"Isn't he studying ancient Greek?" came a voice from behind the newspaper.

"It's almost the same thing," said an impatient Anita. "It's fun, hitch-hiking. You see things, and talk to different people."

"I suppose you don't want to come with us to Wales, then," said her father. He sounded sarcastic.

"Oh, father," said Anita again. "I'm too old for that. I want something different. I can't go and sit on a Welsh beach with you all day. Anyway, you're only going there for two weeks. I've got nine weeks holiday."

"Who said we're going to Wales again? Why don't we all go to Italy?" said her mother in a hurry. "I saw some very nice Venice holidays in Swift's, the travel agents, yesterday."

Anita felt she was in a trap. They wanted to keep her with them all the time.

"Package tours are OK for people like you," she said. "They are for tourists. Rolf and I don't want to be tourists. We want to be free, and meet people from different countries, and talk to them. You can't do that on a package tour."

Her mother was indignant.

"What's wrong with tourists? And what's the difference between us in a tourist bus and you in private cars. More dangerous for you, that's all."

"Hrrmph," said her father.

Both Anita and her mother turned and started to say something furious to him.

"George, this is …"

"Father, can't you …?"

"I wanted to read you something from the newspaper," he said. "It says that two young girls disappeared last week in France. They were hitch-hiking to Montpellier it seems."

Anita took the paper from his hands, and looked for the bit about the two girls.

"Look. It says they were hitch-hiking at night," she said, impatient again. "That's silly. Everyone knows that. Rolf and I are doing it in the day."

"And two girls together is silly," she added. And left the room.

There was a silence. No-one knew what to say. Then George Mitchell put down his newspaper and said to his wife,

"Oh, Helen, I forgot to tell you. I had a letter this morning form Peter Lord. Aunt Ada has died."

"Aunt Ada? Who's she?" asked Helen.

"Aunt Ada? You know Aunt Ada," said George Mitchell, with a tender expression on his face. She's my mad Liverpool aunt who went to be a missionary in New Guinea."

"Oh yes," said his wife, with a laugh. "Didn't she take the cucumber out of our cucumber sandwiches and put it on her forehead in hot weather, saying it was cool?"

"Yes," said George. He didn't remember this, but it was quite possible. Aunts did things like that, especially aunts like Ada.

"I liked her," said Helen, with another laugh. Anita always said her mother had a silly laugh. "She wanted to be friends with cannibals in Africa, but the vicar said there aren't any cannibals in Africa these days. Would she like some headhunters instead? Aunt Ada said yes, so the vicar recommended her to a vicar friend in New Guinea."

She laughed again.

"Yes, I remember Aunt Ada. Mmm. So she's died, has she? Where did she die?"

"In the rain forests somewhere, it seems," said George Mitchell. He got up and went to get the letter. He came back in a minute, with the letter in his hand. "Yes, she died at a place called New Tonga. Mmm."

He read through the letter again, then went on.

"It seems they're burying her in the church there. It seems all her friends from the village will be there."

"The headhunters?"

"Well, yes," said George, with an embarrassed laugh. He looked back at the letter. "Peter thinks it could be a good thing if I go there to the funeral. She hasn't got any other members of her family there; or anywhere else, for that matter."

There was silence again. They didn't know what to say.

"It's a long way," said Helen.

"Mmm," said George. He didn't like long journeys.

"How do you get there?" asked Helen.

A funny expression appeared on her husband's face. He was thinking.

"I don't know," he said after a minute or two. "You go to Australia, don't you?"

"It's expensive," she said.

There was another silence. George Mitchell picked up his paper again, and turned the pages. He found the travel page. It was full of advertisements for flights to Australia, but they weren't cheap.

"Do you think you need to go?" asked his wife. "I don't think you need to go. After all, she was only your aunt."

The funny expression appeared on his face again. He didn't think about his family very often, but Family was Family. And Aunt Ada was Family, too.

"Of course I have to go. She's my family. Would you like to die alone, without a member of your family there?"

"But it's expensive, George," said Helen.

"Hmph," said her husband, and picked up his newspaper again.

At that moment, Anita came through the door and said aggressively, "What about my holiday?"

Her father read his paper, her mother went over to the TV and turned it on.

"There's a good programme on English gardens at 8.30," she said, in a comfortable voice.

"Oh," said Anita. "Your never listen to me."

And she went out of the room.

Her father turned over the last page of his newspaper. At the bottom was a small advertisement: 'Air Niugini', it said. 'Special family tickets to Port Moresby. For this month only, 100 pounds for maximum four members of the same family. Also, cheap tickets for students.'

"Hey," said George. "Helen, look at this. Let's all go to Ada's funeral, and have a holiday at the same time."

His wife came over, looked at the newspaper, and then looked at her husband.

"I don't want a holiday in New Guinea, George. You go, with Anita. You and she can go. I don't mind. I'll go to my mother's in Clacton."

"That's a good idea," said George with enthusiasm. "Anita can come with me. Then she doesn't have to go on that dangerous hitch-hiking thing with her college friend. I'm sure she wants to say goodbye to Aunt Ada, too. Hey, Anita!" he called.

"What?" came a voice from the next room.

"We're going to Aunt Ada's funeral."

Then Helen said, "It's the Cup Final next week, George. What about your ticket for the Cup Final? Can you sell it to someone?"

Anita came back into the room and looked at her father.

"What did you say?"

"Oh, it wasn't anything important, Anita. I'm thinking aloud, that's all."

"Your father and you are going to Aunt Ada's funeral," said Helen. She saw the expression on Anita's face, and added, "It's all right, Anita. Don't be afraid. It's not dangerous there. After all, they do speak English there, don't they?"

Anita looked amazed.

"Um. I don't think I can go," said her father. "I've just remembered. I've got an important meeting with my bank manager next week. But Anita can go alone. I can't see any problems. Can you, Helen?"

"Go where, father?" asked Anita. "Where can I go alone?"

"To New Guinea."

"To New Guinea! Are you quite mad? I'm not going to New Guinea."

"But you wanted a holiday!"

"I suppose you think it's a holiday for me if I go to a funeral in New Guinea. Well, I'm not. I'm going to Clacton."

Her mother's mouth fell open in surprise.

"To Clacton? Why Clacton? What gave you that idea?"

"Grandmother has invited Rolf and me to stay with her. I've just spoken to her on the phone."

"My mother has done what?!" said Helen.

"Oh, don't worry, mother. It's not dangerous there. They do speak English in Clacton, after all."

Her mother found her voice again.

"But you can't go to my mother's house with a boy friend," she said.

"Why not?" asked Anita.

"People don't do things like that. Anyway, you're too young."

"No, I'm not. I'm 18 next month. I can do what I want." And she went out of the room and closed the door behind her.

When In Rome, Do As The Romans Do

John and Betty German were (despite their name) very English. Even when they went abroad, they were always sure to wait for the other person to speak, before they spoke; they were reserved; they tried to become part of the landscape – they didn't like noise and they hated it if other people noticed them. They wanted to be invisible tourists.

"When in Rome," they said, "it's best to do as the Romans do."

This year, they went to Scandinavia. Everyone said Scandinavia is like England. English people can understand Scandinavian languages without much difficulty, they said. Scandinavians are so much like the English, really.

To John and Betty German, this did not seem at all true, however. When they arrived in Copenhagen, they listened and looked, but said nothing. When you are abroad, they said, the first rule is: listen and look. See what people do. Then do the same.

Well, the language was a bit of a problem. Danish is like English in one or two ways. The most important way: you don't say what you write. That is about the only similarity.

John and Betty didn't understand a word. So they took out their dictionaries, and tried to become good Danish speakers.

The Danes listened with a polite expression, then said in English, "You're from England, I expect. Do you like it here?"

Oh well, perhaps they only know one sentence. After all, people say that in every country – "Do you like it here?" The next question after that is usually "How long are you staying here?" If you're staying only one day, it can be an insult. If you're staying two weeks, you're obviously a tourist of good taste. You obviously understand that this is an Important Country.

John and Betty German tried it a different way. They took out their Danish dictionaries again and said,

"Herlig vejr."

(In England, they thought, you always talk about the weather with your friends and neighbours, not with tourists.)

"Mmm. Lovely weather. The weather is usually very good at this time of year. Have you been to Denmark before at this time of the year?" asked the Danes in excellent English. (The English always talk about the weather, they thought. If you want to be polite with English people, always talk about the weather.)

Oh dear, thought John and Betty. It isn't easy to do as the Romans do. What do the Romans do next? Ah. They talk about illnesses. Let's try that.

John took out his dictionary and looked up the words for: "When the weather changes, people often get headaches." (There was now a cloud in the sky.)

Unfortunately, he couldn't find a good Danish expression for that, so he pointed at the cloud and put his hands to his head.

The Danes looked at the painful face he was making. He's not very well, they thought. I expect he's got a headache. "Oh, you poor man," they said in English. "You need some aspirin. There's a chemist at the next corner."

Well, that was enough for one day; they thanked their Danish friends for their help and went on their way. For the moment John and Betty wanted to be invisible tourists again. They were going to look at the porno shops in the Nygade. Everyone said they were very interesting, because people in Denmark were so uninhibited about things like that. Not like in England. In England, only dirty old men in long, dirty raincoats go to shops like that. In Denmark, everybody goes there, people said.

Well, anyway, they saw the porno shops, but there weren't many Danes in them; so they thought, perhaps we're a bit visible here. The place is full of dirty young men in jeans from other countries. So they decided to go on an excursion into the country. Not in a tourist bus, but by train. The trains are very good in Denmark, and you can see the country from the train.

It was Sunday. They got off the train at a little country station, where there were just a few houses and a lovely little church. They walked round the village and said 'goddei' to the friendly faces in the houses, then went into the church. At home, they usually went to church on Sundays, and they saw that the next service was starting in about twenty minutes. People were already arriving for the service. They decided to stay. They didn't know the service in Danish, so they decided to sit down and do everything that the people in front of them did.

They sat down in the middle of the church and waited. After another ten minutes, the church was almost full. A very respectable couple came and sat down in front of them. John and Betty fastened their gaze on this couple, and did everything they did. When the service started and the couple got up, they got up, too. When the couple sat down, they sat down too. They even tried to sing.

The plan worked very well. John and Betty felt quite at home. But, after a time, the pastor got up and in a quiet voice said a few words to the congregation. Then he took out a little book and read something out of it. The Danish couple stood up. At once John and Betty German got up too. To their horror, everybody else in the church stayed seated. John and Betty sat down again, their ears red with embarrassment. At the end of the service, they left in a great hurry. They tried not to look at the faces of the other people in the congregation.

Later, back at the station, they met someone who was also at the service, the station-master. He explained to them, "First, the pastor always reads out the notices. Then he reads out news of christenings, and things like that. Today he told us about Mr and Mrs Jespersen's little boy. They were sitting in front of you. The christening is tomorrow, and he asked the proud parents to stand up. For a moment we all thought the little Jespersen boy had four parents!" Just then, the train arrived. John and Betty were very glad to get into it.

The train whistled and started. John and Betty German looked out of the window as the train left the station. The village looked almost like an English village.

The station-master waved at them.

A Most Unusual Journey

A not-so-young businessman was on a flight from London to New York. At the best of times, he was not a very good traveller, and this journey was a bad one. The wind was strong, and the plane went up and down for hours. After a time, the businessman felt so ill that he had to get up from his seat, and stagger down to the toilet at the back of the plane.

While he was being sick into the toilet, his false teeth fell out of his mouth and into the metal bowl of the aircraft toilet. For a moment, he did not notice, and he pressed the button of the toilet, to flush it.

As it flushed, he saw his false teeth. The water carried them away, out of sight behind the metal trap in the toilet.

The passenger was desperate to get his teeth back. He plunged his arm into the bowl and pushed his hand behind the metal trap, trying to reach the false teeth. He wasn't able to reach them.

The trouble started when he tried to take his arm out of toilet again. The metal trap held his arm fast – the design of the trap stopped the backward movement of things into the bowl.

In despair, the passenger pressed the button for the steward, and soon a steward and a stewardess were at the door. They opened the door, and found a man with his arm up to the shoulder in the toilet.

They tried their best to pull the man's arm out of the toilet, but they too were unable to do so. So the plane went on its way, and landed at John Fitzgerald Kennedy Airport in New York, with a passenger kneeling at the back of the aircraft with his arm in a toilet. An hour or two after the arrival of the plane, engineers were able to cut his arm out at last.

At The Enquiries Desk

Clerk: Good morning, madam. Can I help you?

Old lady: Yes. I want to book a flight to Spain. And I need your advice, because it's my very first flight, you know. I'm 79, so I have to be careful, you see.

Clerk: But that's fantastic, madam. I'm glad you're so interested in foreign travel still.

Old lady: Thank you, young man. Of course, at my age, plane fares seem absurdly expensive. But this trip is a present to me from my son. I'm 80 in June, you see.

Clerk: That's very nice for you, madam. Now, let's see. When do you want to travel?

Old lady: In June, of course. My son says I must spend my birthday with him and his wife. He lives there, you see.

Clerk: Ah, I understand. Now what …?

Old lady: Yes, he's been there for twenty years now. He went to Malaga on a trip. He was selling biscuits at that time, I think. Yes, it was biscuits. Neece biscuits.

Clerk: I understand entirely, madam. He was selling nice biscuits. Now, can we …?

Old lady: No, No. Nice biscuits, young man. Like Nice in France, you know. Well, then he met this Spanish girl, um … Mary.

Clerk: So now you're going to Spain to visit him and his wife, er, Maria?

Old lady: His wife's name is Mary. Didn't I say? Her father was Irish.

29

Clerk: Right, madam. Now. You want to fly to Spain in June, to visit your son and his Spanish-Irish wife Mary.

Old lady: That's right, young man. You're very intelligent. That's just what I want. Except that ... Mary's mother is Mexican, not Spanish.

Clerk: I'm sorry, madam. My mistake. Now. What time of the day did you want to travel?

Old lady: Oh, it must be during the day. I want to get there during the day. I've never seen her, you see. He's never brought her to England on holiday. So I want to see her when I get there. First impressions are very important. Don't you agree?

Clerk: Oh, entirely, madam. Now, let me look at the ABC. Mmm. There are several direct flights from Heathrow to Spain, and they all arrive before 6. It isn't dark there until after six. So that's no problem. Right. Did you want to book a return ticket?

Old lady: Oh, no. Certainly not. Just one way. My son can buy the return ticket for me over there. I'm sure he can do that. He can speak very good Spanish, he says in his letters. I expect they can understand him at the Spanish travel agent. And if he can't speak Spanish, I'm sure they can understand his wife Mary. She's Spanish, you know. Didn't I say?

Clerk: Yes, madam. You also said that your son is paying for your trip. So it's cheaper for him if you buy a return ticket here, you know.

Old lady: No. Out of the question. He hasn't sent me any money yet. If he forgets to give it to me when I'm there ... well, I can always live with him until he

	gives it to me. If I've got a return ticket, I have to come home. No, it's out of the question.

Clerk: As you wish, madam. Now, would you like a hotel? Hotels in Spain are often air-conditioned, and they are usually very comfortable, so ...

Old lady: No, certainly not. I must stay with my son and see if this girl is really looking after him or not.

Clerk: Right, madam. Can I just write that down? Er ... 'no accommodation'. Right. Now, which airline do you want to fly with?

Old lady: A British airline, of course. It must be British. I have to talk to the stewardesses, don't I?

Clerk: But, madam! The stewardesses on all these planes speak excellent English, and you can explain ...

Old lady: No, no. You never know for sure. Book me on a British plane.

Clerk: Certainly, madam. Right, I think I've written down everything. A single ticket to Spain from Heathrow, in June. No accomodation. A British airline with a day-time direct flight. Now, just one small thing ... Where exactly do you want to go?

Old lady: Don't be so impertinent and curious, young man. You just give me a ticket to Spain, and stop all these silly questions!

First Stop Mars

Passport O.K. Health certificate O.K. Trade certificate ... baggage O.K. No special personal features. Visas O.K. Ticket O.K.

With an uninterested expression on his face, the official looked through Daren's papers, and then gave them back to him.

"Which way?" asked Daren.

"The shuttle takes off from Station 35. You go through Gate 6. Your ticket will glow as long as you're going the right way."

The shuttle looked small, but it wasn't. Daren took his turn in the queue for the lift. Soon, he was moving up in the lift with four other people. The doors opened, and they entered the cabin of the shuttle.

"I'm glad we don't have to go all the way in this thing," said one of the men who was with him in the lift, as they sat down. "How long can they go on with these old shuttles? Spindizzy's the thing. That's the way to travel. It's got to come."

"What's that?" asked Daren. He wasn't really interested. He didn't like any sort of travel.

"Anti-gravity. They've got to have it one day. Then the ships can come right down."

"I suppose spaceships are too big." Daren tried to sound intelligent about it. "I know they build them out in space, not down here."

"Haven't you ever seen one? They're huge."

The man looked at him.

"What do you do? he asked.

"I'm a bio-chemist," said Daren.

"Then you must work in the Plantlife Promotion Laboratory."

"That's right. Do you work there too?"

"No. I'm from Maintenance. I look after the plastic domes we live in until there's a proper atmosphere. If there ever is a proper atmosphere! Hello. We're off!"

Daren felt his stomach fall into his boots. Several other passengers were holding their stomachs. He wondered if it helped. He tried it, and it did help.

Everybody was quiet. After a few minutes, their stomachs started to return to their bodies, as the shuttle moved slower. Instead, it started to sway and dip, like a ship. Only the belt held him in his seat. He felt awful. He couldn't say which way up he was, and he felt quite sick. He hoped they would arrive before his stomach betrayed him.

"Is it like this all the way?" he asked.

"No," said the maintenance man, aggressive. Daren wondered if he too felt sick. "On the ship there's artificial gravity, so you walk like here. No problem."

"Thank heavens for that."

"Thank science, you mean. In the old days, when there were flights to the moon and Mars, everybody floated all the time. I expect it was awful."

"It was," said a very old man with silver hair over his thin face. "I was an astronaut. We didn't like it at all."

"Are you really that old?" asked a young passenger, amazed. Daren suddenly felt terribly sick again. The man in the next chair said in a friendly voice,

"It doesn't last long. This part of the trip, I mean. They keep the ship quite close to the atmosphere."

"Can you keep quiet?" said another passenger behind them. His face was pale, and Daren could see perspiration on his forehead. "There are too many people in this shuttle, and you're using up oxygen."

"Sorry," said Daren. The man next to him didn't say anything for a minute or two, then said,

"Don't take any notice of him," with a movement of his head towards the pale face behind them. "He's just afraid. It's not oxygen he needs. It's guts."

Suddenly there was a noise on one side, and the shuttle shook like a leaf. The movement threw all the passengers against their belts.

"We're locking on," said a voice.

"That's quick," said another.

"What do we do now?" asked Daren. He tried to open the buckle of his belt.

"Don't do that yet," said his neighbour. "If you don't keep your belt on, you float around and kick everybody. Wait until the door opens. Then, when it's your turn, you can float through into the ship."

"I thought there was gravity on the ship."

"So there is. But we're not in the ship yet. Wait until you're through the airlock."

At last the big, round, heavy door swung open. One by one, the people in the shuttle swam through the door and along a tunnel.

Daren wasn't ready when it was his turn, and didn't know what to do. He didn't put his feet down like a swimmer in a swimming pool. He fell forward, and landed on his face. A hand under his arm helped him to get up.

"First time?"

A friendly face looked down at him. It was an official from the Spaceship Company. He nodded.

The official said, "It's better the second time."

He made a movement with his head towards a room just inside the ship.

"The canteen's in there. You can look for a cabin if you want, but there's no hurry. Several other shuttles have to arrive here first."

Daren wasn't hungry. He wandered off, down towards the huge main room of the spaceship. In every direction, corridors ran off from the main room. People talked and moved, and did what they were doing in a sort of strange silence. There was a quiet hum in the main room, the noise of the huge power system. Lift doors opened, people came out of the lifts, and the doors closed again in silence. Other people got into lifts, which took them away to other parts of the huge ship. It was almost like a city. Daren wondered where the control rooms were. He wondered if passengers ever went into the control rooms. He would like to see them, he thought.

"It's a bit frightening, don't you think?"

Daren looked round. A pretty girl with a crown of red-gold hair was standing near him.

"Yes," he said. "But it's exciting, too. Don't you agree?" Daren couldn't take his eyes off her. She really was lovely.

"I suppose that's quite true," she said. "I expect you've travelled before."

Daren wanted to say yes, but didn't. It was better not to.

"Actually, no. This is my first flight. Is it yours, too?"

"Yes. I've just finished my studies. I'm a botanist."

"Oh, good. I expect to see you at the Plantlife Promotion Laboratory, then."

"Is that where you work?"

"Yes. I'm a bio-chemist. I hope they send you there. It's a nice place to work."

He said the words more with hope than expectation. She was so lovely. It wasn't possible that a pretty girl like that was unattached.

"Perhaps," she agreed. But her eyes seemed to hold a strange laugh in them. He saw that her eyes were a funny green-blue colour, the colour of deep sea in sunshine. Something inside him jumped when he saw that little laugh in them. Perhaps it wasn't a bad trip after all. She was a friend, he thought.

"My name's Daren," he said. "Daren Smith."

"I'm Jessica Tarrant."

"What about something to eat, Jessica?" Suddenly he felt quite hungry.

"I think I must go and find a cabin first. It's a long journey, and I don't want to have to stand."

They turned to go.

"They say the cabins are really only a sort of cubicle thing."

They walked off together. As they went, Daren saw that the men were looking at Jessica and then at him. Were they envious? He hoped so. He looked to his right, down at her lovely crown of hair. Was she more than 20? It wasn't possible. He was only 21, after all. He was six feet tall. As they walked, he felt taller.

As they came nearer, doors opened without a noise. Signs glowed, and arrows pointed out that they were going towards the sleeping quarters for passengers. On other doors there were signs saying "Keep Out" in many languages.

The cabins were quite big after all. In each there were two bunks, behind thick curtains.

"Would you ...?" Daren couldn't finish the sentence.

I'd love to," said Jessica, in her clear voice. "I'll have the one below."

They each left one or two things on their bunks, to show they were coming back. The other passengers were doing the same in the other cabins. Then, together, they went to the purser's office, where they registered their cabin.

"You two together?" asked the purser, but he did not seem to expect an answer to his question. He turned round as they came in, but did not put his book down.

"For the trip," said Jessica.

Daren wondered what she meant. He tried to see the expression on her face, but she was looking at the purser. Then they were outside again in the corridor.

Soon, life on the ship became a routine. People ate, slept, played cards or talked. People became friends. Others became enemies. Others sat and didn't do anything.

The friendship with Jessica didn't change. She didn't become more friendly. But, then again, she didn't become less friendly. Most of the other women on the spaceship seemed to have partners already. And, although there were about four men on the ship for each woman, the three unlucky men did not seem to try to steal partners from the one lucky one. Because people saw Jessica and Daren together even on the first day, they accepted that they did most things together and went places together. Jessica stayed friendly but cool; but they played cards together and spent long hours together in the observation room. It was a comfortable arrangement, and Daren, despite his age, was a patient man.

When Jessica was not with him, Daren spent all his time in the observation room. It seemed to him a wonderful place. He wondered if he could do the job of a spaceman. Of course, this was his first trip, but there were so many psychological adjustments before he would feel at home. He looked out through the window and saw Mother Earth, a bright blue ball in the dark sky. It was becoming smaller, and soon was like a pinhead of light. It was almost painful.

"It is painful," said a voice near him, putting his thought into words. "Earth is our mother. When we leave Earth, it is like a new birth for us." She watched Daren's face. She was a tall, dark woman, about 45 years old. Later, Daren found out that she was a Professor of Psychology, and was going to Mars for a second tour of duty.

"Yes," said Daren. He hoped that the feeling at the back of his head wasn't turning to tears. But, just then, Jessica moved close to him, and her arm touched his. The feeling of loneliness left him.

"Let's go down," she said. She wasn't interested in Earth. It was Mars that interested her.

"Let's," said Daren.

Then, all too soon, the flight was over. Quiet voices on the intercom said that the ship was going round Mars for a time.

"For those people on their first trip to Mars, this is your first chance to look at Planet Mars," said the intercom.

Soon there were crowds in the observation room. The ship moved between darkness and sunshine as it went round the planet. Daren heard comments on all sides.

"It looks barren," said one voice.

"It looks awful," said another. "What about water?"

"They're trying to find some," said another. "Anyway, we've brought a lot with us."

"That can't last long," said the first voice with a laugh.

"No problem," said the third voice. "They recycle all the water. Once, twice, three times, if we need it."

"Ugh," said a woman.

"Over there," said a man's voice in Daren's right ear.

"That's where you'll be working. That's the laboratory."

He pointed out a large area in the middle of the window.

It was the maintenance man from the shuttle. Daren saw little of him during the trip. Most of the time, the maintenance man played cards with a few friends in a corner of the Games Room, or in the bars.

"Do we wear space suits when we go from one building to another?" asked Daren.

"Yes," said the man. He looked at Jessica. "Lucky man. Nice chick, eh?"

He winked.

Jessica turned as she heard him. Her eyes flashed. The maintenance man made a small wave of the hand to Daren, turned and went out with a laugh.

"Come on," said Daren, "it's time to go down."

He hoped she didn't take it as an insult. She could refuse to talk to him.

But she didn't say anything, just walked in front of him into the airlock to the shuttle.

This time it was not so difficult. Daren floated in a minute into his place in the shuttle. Soon, the shuttle was locking on to a huge tower on Mars.

Again, they had to use the airlock to get out, but this time they could walk down through the tunnel. They didn't have to swim. They went into the tower, and lifts took them down to the ground.

"Will I see you?" Daren asked in desperation. He saw that his sign was different from hers. His was red, hers was green, and pointed to a different part of the area.

"I expect so."

She looked at him with a friendly expression, and moved on. He went to the back of the line of people with red tickets. It was over. The long, strange journey. The end of one life and, for a year or two, the beginning of another. He looked down the long corridor. In the distance he could see a crown of red-gold hair, glowing like a star. It gave him some hope for the future.

"Ticket, please."

Daren held out his red ticket. The sudden feeling of loneliness left him.

He took a step forward.

Anne Pewsey

Robinson Crusoe's Diary

September 30th, 1659. I, poor miserable Robinson Crusoe, shipwrecked during a terrible storm, have arrived on this unhappy island – I call it the Island of Despair. The others of the ship's company all died at sea.

All the rest of these last days I have thought only of my unhappy condition: now I have no food, no house, no clothes, no weapon nor anywhere to go; and in my despair I see nothing but death before me. Perhaps wild animals will eat me, or savages will kill me, or I will die of hunger. Last night I slept in a tree, afraid of wild animals; but I slept well, even though it rained all night.

October 1st. In the morning, I saw to my great surprise that the ship was much nearer the island, carried in with the high tide. This was a great comfort to me, because she was upright and in one piece. When the wind became less strong, I hoped I could go on board, and get some food and other things out of her. On the other hand, I remembered again my dead comrades, and thought that, if we were still all on the ship, we would all be alive. I spent the great part of the day on these unhappy thoughts; but at last I saw that the ship was almost dry. I went on the sand, as near as I could, and then swam to the ship. Today it also rained, but there was no wind.

1st October–24th October. All these days I went out to the ship and back, to get everything possible out of the ship. I brought all the things on to the beach, with each high tide, on rafts. There was a lot of rain during these days, though several times there was good weather in between. But it seems this is the rainy season.

October 20th. I upset my raft and all the things on it, but, because it was not deep water and the things were mostly heavy, I was able to get them all back when the tide was out.

October 25th. It rained all night and all day, with some wind. The wind and the sea broke the ship into pieces, leaving only the wreck behind, and this I could see only at low tide. Today I tied down and covered the things which I brought from the ship. I am afraid that the rain will spoil them.

October 26th. I walked about the shore almost all day, to find out a place for my home. I must have a place where I can be safe from an attack in the night, from wild animals or from men. Towards night, I decided on a place under a rock. I drew a half-circle for my camp. On this half-circle I decided to build a wall of double timber piles, and inside them timber spars, outside earth.

From the 26th to the 30th. I worked very hard to carry all my goods to my new home. Some of the time it rained very hard.

October 31st. This morning I went out into the island with my gun and looked for food. I wanted also to look around the country. I killed a she-goat, and the baby goat followed me home. This I afterwards killed, too, because it did not want to eat.

November 1st. I built my tent under a rock. Here I spent the first night. I made the place as big as possible, with piles in the ground – on these I hung my hammock.

November 2nd. I built my chests and shelves from the pieces of timber from my rafts. With them, I made a fence around me, too, just inside the place where I decided to build my wall.

November 3rd. I went out with my gun and killed two birds like ducks – they were very good food. In the afternoon, I started work on a table.

November 4th. This morning I began to organise my times of work – the times when I go out with my gun, the times when I sleep, the times when I relax. Now, every morning I walk out with my gun for two or three hours, when it is not raining; then, until about eleven, I work; then I eat what I have; and from twelve to two I lie down to sleep, because the weather is very hot; then in the evening I work again. The working part of this day and of the next, I spent with my table. I am still not a very good workman. Time will of course make me better.

November 5th.   Today I went out with my gun and my dog, and killed a wild cat. Her skin is quite soft, but there is no meat on her. I take off the skins of all the creatures that I kill, and I keep them. As I was coming back along the shore, I saw a lot of different kinds of sea-bird. Also, I saw two or three seals, which alarmed me. While I was looking at them, not knowing what they were, they got into the sea and escaped me.

November 6th.   After my morning walk, I went to work with my table again, and finished it, though it is not very good. Soon I found out how to make a better one.

November 7th.   Now it has begun to be good weather. I spent the days from the 7th to the 12th (but not the 11th, a Sunday) with a new chair. After a lot of work and trouble, I made quite a good chair; but it did not please me, and I pulled it in pieces several times. Soon I forgot to write the days on my post, and I did not keep my Sundays after that.

* * *

July 14th.   I have now been on this unhappy island for more than 10 months. It does not seem possible that I will ever leave this island. I do not believe that humans ever set foot on this island.

Daniel Defoe

The Final Problem

"You will spend the night here, Holmes?" I said.

"No, Watson; you would find me a dangerous guest. I have my plans – all will be well. Things are so far now that the police can move without my help and make an arrest, though I shall have to be there in court later. No, I cannot do better than get away for the remaining few days before the police are free to act. It would be a great pleasure to me, therefore, if you could come to the Continent with me."

"I do not have many appointments this week," I said, "and I have a helpful neighbour. I should be glad to come."

"And to start tomorrow morning?"

"If necessary."

"Oh yes, it is very necessary. Then this is what you have to do, and I must ask you, my dear Watson, to do *exactly* what I say. You are now playing a double-handed game with me against the cleverest rogue and the most powerful group of criminals in Europe. Now listen! You will send your luggage with your man to Victoria Station – it will have no address on it. In the morning you will call a cab, but your man must not take the first or second cab which arrives. You will get into the cab, and you will drive to the Strand end of the Lowther Arcade – you will give the address to the cabman on a piece of paper, asking him not to throw it away. Have your fare ready, and the moment when your cab stops, run through the Arcade, so that you get to the other side at a quarter-past nine. You will find a small brougham waiting at the side of the road. The driver will be a fellow with a heavy black cloak with a red collar. Into this you will jump, and you will get to Victoria in time for the Continental express."

"Where shall I meet you?"

"At the station. I shall reserve for us the second first-class carriage from the front."

"We meet at the carriage, then?"

"Yes."

I asked Holmes again to stay for the evening, but he refused. It was clear to me that he thought it was dangerous for me if he stayed, and that was why he wanted to leave. After a few more words about our plan for the next day, he got up and came out with me into the garden, climbed over the wall which looks on to Mortimer Street, and at once called for a cab. I heard him drive away.

In the morning, I did exactly what Holmes told me. I found a cab which could not possibly be waiting for me. I drove at once after breakfast to the Lowther Arcade, and ran through the Arcade as fast as I could. A brougham was waiting with a very large driver in a dark cloak; and as soon as I got in, he whipped up the horse and we hurried to Victoria Station. When I got out there, he turned the cab and hurried away without a look in my direction.

So far so good. My baggage was waiting for me, and I easily found our carriage – it was the only one in the train which had 'Reserved' on it. My only problem now was, where was Holmes? It was only seven minutes (by the station clock) to the time when the train would leave. I looked among the groups of travellers for my friend, but there was no sign of him. For a few minutes, I helped an old Italian priest, who was trying to explain, in bad English, to a porter that his baggage was going direct to Paris. After that I took another look round and went back to my carriage, where I found that the porter, despite the RESERVED notice, was putting my old Italian friend in with me. I tried to explain to him that I did not want him in my compartment, but my Italian was worse even than his English, so I sat down with a shrug, and looked anxiously out of the window for my friend. A cold feeling of fear came over me. I thought that, because he was not there, something was wrong – something that happened during the night. The doors were already shutting, the train was just leaving when –

"My dear Watson," said a voice, "when are you going to say good morning to me?"

I turned in astonishment. The old priest was looking at me. For a moment the wrinkles disappeared, the mouth stopped mumbling, the dull eyes became interesting and the old figure filled out with strength. In the next moment, the whole body collapsed, and Holmes was there no more.

"Good heavens!" I called. "You startled me."

"We have to be absolutely careful," he whispered. "I think they are not far behind us. Ah, there is Moriarty himself."

The train was already moving when Holmes said these words. I looked back and saw a tall man push through the crowd furiously. He was waving his hand, and it was clear that he wanted to stop the train. But it was too late. The train was going quite fast, and a moment later was outside the station.

"Did you see the morning paper, Watson?"

"No."

"You didn't see about Baker Street, then?"

"Baker Street?"

"They set fire to our rooms last night. The rooms were not much damaged."

"Good heavens, Holmes! We cannot put up with this."

"I expect they lost track of me when their strongman fell into the hands of the police. Otherwise they could not think that I was in my rooms. But they *did* take the trouble to watch you, and that is why Moriarty is here in Victoria. You did not make any mistakes on the way to Victoria?"

"I did exactly what you told me."
"Did you find your brougham?"
"Yes, it was waiting."
"Did you recognize your coachman?"
"No."
"It was my brother Mycroft. At times like this, it is helpful to get about without the use of paid helpers. But we must think what we are going to do about Moriarty now."
"This is an express. The boat connects with it. I think he will not be able to follow us."
"My dear Watson, I do not think you completely understood me when I said that this man is for practical purposes on the same intellectual plane as I am. If I were in his place, you cannot think this would be a problem to me? Why do you think it will be a problem to him?"
"What will he do?"
"What I should do."
"What would you do, then?"
"Take a special train."
"But it must be late."
"Not at all. This train stops at Canterbury; and there is always a quarter of an hour's wait at the boat. He will catch us there."
"It would almost seem that *we* are the criminals. Cannot the police arrest him when he arrives?"
"That would ruin three months' work. We would catch the small fish, but miss the bigger fish completely. On Monday we shall have them all. No, an arrest is not possible."
"What then?"
"We shall get out at Canterbury."
"And then?"
"Well, then we must make a cross-country journey to Newhaven, and so over to Dieppe. Moriarty will again do what I

should do. He will get on to Paris, look for our baggage, and wait for two days in the baggage office. In the meantime, we shall buy two large bags, and other things, in the countries through which we travel, and make our way to Switzerland, via Luxembourg and Basle."

I am too old a traveller that I should be really worried to lose my baggage; but I admit it annoyed me that Holmes wanted to hide before a man who was such a desperate criminal. But it was clear that Holmes understood the situation better than I did. At Canterbury, therefore, we got out, and found that we had to wait an hour for a train to Newhaven.

I was watching regretfully the bagagge car of the train as it disappeared over the horizon with my clothes when Holmes pulled at my sleeve and pointed out something up the line.

"Already, you see," he said.

A long way away, behind the woods of Kent, was a thin cloud of smoke. A minute later, a carriage and engine came into sight at great speed. We hardly had time to hide behind a pile of baggage when it roared through the station with a cloud of hot air and smoke.

"There he goes," said Holmes, as we watched the carriage swing and rock over the points. "There are, you see, limits to our friend's intelligence. He should *know* that I know what he thinks, and he should act differently. There is no doubt that he intends to murder me. But that is a game that two can play. The question now is, do we have an early lunch here, or shall we take a chance of starving before we get to the buffet at Newhaven?"

We made our way to Brussels that night, and spent two days there. On the third day, we moved on to Strasburg. On the Monday morning, Holmes sent a telegram to the London police, and in the evening we found a reply waiting for us at our hotel. Holmes opened it in a hurry, then with a bitter curse threw it furiously into the fire.

"I knew it," he muttered. "He escaped!"

"Moriarty!"

"They caught the whole gang, but not him. He escaped. Of course, when I left the country, there was no-one who could deal with him. But I did think that I put the game in their hands. I think it would be best if you go back to England, Watson."

"Why?"

"Because you will find me a dangerous companion now. This man has nothing else to live for. He is lost if he goes back to London. If I read him right, he will turn all his energies to revenge – on me. Indeed, that was what he said when we met, and I think that he was sincere. I should certainly recommend that you go back to your appointments in London."

It was hardly the sort of thing to say to someone who was an old comrade-in-arms, as well as an old friend. We sat in the Strasburg salle-à-manger and argued the question for half an hour, but the same night we continued our journey and were soon on our way to Geneva.

For a delightful week, we wandered up the Valley of the Rhône, and then made our way over the Gemmi Pass, still deep in snow, and so, via Interlaken, to Meiringen. It was a lovely trip; but it was clear to me that, never for one moment, did Holmes forget the shadow which lay across him. In the Alpine villages and in the lonely passes, I could still tell, as he looked at every face that went past, that he thought that, in every place we went, we could not walk ourselves clear of the danger that walked behind us.

And yet, for all this, he was never depressed. Again and again he went back to the fact that, if he knew that society could be free of Professor Moriarty, he would happily bring his own career to an end.

"I think I may say, Watson, that my life was not without meaning," he said. "The air of London is sweeter for my presence. In over a thousand cases, I do not think I ever used my powers on the wrong side. And your memoirs will come to an end, Watson, on the day that I crown my career with the capture of the most dangerous and clever criminal in Europe."

There is little that is left to tell. It was on May 3rd that we arrived at the little village of Meiringen, where we stayed at the Englischer Hof. The landlord was Peter Steiler. At his advice, on the afternoon of the 4th, we set off towards the hills. We wanted to spend the night at the small village of Rosenlaui. He told us not on any account to miss a visit to the falls of Reichenbach, which are about half way up the hill.

It is, indeed, a terrible place. The path is cut halfway round the falls, so that you can see them. But it stops suddenly, and the visitor has to go back the way he came. We were turning to go back when we saw a Swiss boy come running. He had a letter in his hand. It had the sign of the hotel on it, and was from the landlord to me. It seemed that, a few minutes after we left, an English lady arrived. She was very ill, and had few hours to live. She would like to see an English doctor, and if I would return, etc. etc.

I had to go back, of course. It was not possible to refuse the request of a fellow-countrywoman who was dying in a foreign country. Yet I did not want to leave Holmes. In the end, my friend would stay some little time at the fall, while I went back to Meiringen. We would meet later in the evening, at Rosenlaui. As I turned away, I saw Holmes with his back against a rock. His arms were folded, and he was looking down into the furious waters. It was the last time that I would ever see him in this world.

Sir Arthur Conan Doyle

Anecdotes

I was on the French boat *Tage*. It was at anchor in the Dardanelles, on Friday 30th April, 1880. There were many Mohammedans on the boat. When prayer-time came, they took out their prayer-rugs and put them out on the deck, with their heads towards Mecca. Just as they began to pray, the current moved the boat, and it began to swing; when they looked up, they saw that they were looking the wrong way. So they turned round and put their rugs straight. And then, of course, the same thing happened again. And it happened again and again, until their prayers were over.

***

I went to Lourdes in 1894, and saved myself more than one pound fourteen shillings. I wanted to go to Gavarnie, in the Pyrenees, and I found that the fare to Lourdes is less than the fare to Pau (but Pau is nearer to Paris, and Lourdes is nearer Gavarnie than Lourdes is). Zola's book *Lourdes* was in fashion then; and I took it with me on my journey, and read it in on the train. On the train, I had to hold it up to the window, because it was quite dark in the compartment. Obviously the book was like poison to everyone else who was going to Lourdes, because I had the compartment to myself. When we got to Lourdes, I bought the antidote that was in the bookshop there – *The Complete Answer to Monsieur Zola's book LOURDES*. But the antidote was not as strong as the poison.

In the Middle Ages, it was the fashion to bring back earth from the Holy Land, which people put on their graves. And there is still a fashion to bring back water from the river Jordan, for use at baptisms. In 1882, I was down by the river Jordan with my mother and a friend of mind, and she said we must bring back some water. So we filled some empty soda-water bottles from this not very nice river. A year or two later, there was a baptism in the family of a friend, and she sent a bottle for use at the baptism. But they did not baptise the child with Jordan water after all. When they opened the bottle, there was so strong a smell that they had to pour the water down the sink.

***

They tell this story of a place near here: the master of the house was dead and in his grave, but he still came home every night and walked about the house. His family thought that the parson should do something about it; and one night the parson came, and threw some earth from near the church on the face of the dead man. At this, the dead man became a black pony. (In these stories, earth from near the church always makes black creatures of some kind out of ghosts; but the black creature is not always as nice as a Dartmoor pony.) They found a rope, and told a boy that he should run with the pony down the side of the valley as fast as he could, and jump across the river Wrey with it. The boy did this; but when he jumped, he found he had only the rope in his hand, and no pony. Ghosts cannot cross water; and this ghost of a pony ran down the hill so fast that it could not stop. It had to try to jump across the water, and when it did, it disappeared.

Cecil Torr

Word List

absurd unsinnig
accept hinnehmen; auf sich nehmen
accommodation Hotelunterkunft
across auf
act handeln
adjustment Anpassung
admire bewundern
admit zugeben
advertisement Werbeanzeige
afraid Angst(haben)
age Alter
aggressive aggressiv
alive lebendig
along durch; auf
although obwohl
amazed erstaunt
among zwischen; unter
anchor auf Anker
annoy ärgern
anti-gravity Gegenschwerkraft
antidote Gegengift
anxious unruhig
anyone irgend jemand
appointment Verabredung
argue besprechen
arm Arm
army Armee
arrange verabreden
arrangement Vereinbarung

arrest verhaften
arrival Ankunft
arrow Pfeil
artificial künstlich
asian Asiat
astonishment Erstaunen
atmosphere Luft
attack Angriff

bad schlecht
ball Ball
bang Knall
banknote Geldschein
baptism Taufe
barren öde
beside neben
betray Verrat begehen
birth Geburt
birthday Geburtstag
biscuit Keks
board Bord
body Körper
bomb Bombe
boot Kofferraum; Stiefel
border Grenze
botanist Botaniker
bowl Schlüssel
boy Junge
brougham Limousine
buckle Schnalle

53

build bauen
bunk Koje
bury beerdigen
businessman Geschäftsmann
button Knopf

cab Taxi
cannibal Kanibale
canteen Kantine
careful vorsichtig
cargo Ladung
carriage Waggon
casual ungezwungen
catch abfangen
chance Gelegenheit
chaos Chaos
chemist Apotheker
chest Kiste
christening Taufe
clever schlau
climb klettern
cloak Umhang, Cape
close schließen
clothes Kleidung
cloud Wolke
coast Küste
collar Kragen
colleague Kollege
colonel Oberst
comfortable angenehm
companion Gefährte
company Mannschaft, Gesellschaft
compartment Abteil
comrade Kamerad

comrade-in-arms Kriegskamerad
concert Konzert
condition Lage
congratulations Glückwünsche
congregation Gemeinde
connect with Anschluß haben
continent Europa
control kontrollieren
corridor Flur
country Land
country people Bauern
couple Paar
court Gericht
cover bedecken
creature Gestalt; Tier
criminal Verbrecher
cross überqueren
cross-country quer durchs Land
crown of hair Haarschopf
cry weinen
cubicle Zelle
cucumber Gurke
cup final Endpokal
curious neugierig
current Strömung
curtain Vorhang
cut out befreien

dance Tanzabend
danger Gefahr
dangerous gefährlich
dardanelles Dardanellen
daughter Tochter
dead tot

deal with fertig werden mit jem.
death Tod
decide beschließen
depressed niedergeschlagen
design Bauart
despair Verzweiflung
desperation Verzweiflung
despite trotz
detail Einzelheit
developing country Entwicklungsland
die sterben
different anders; unterschiedlich
difficulty Schwierigkeit
direction Richtung
disappear verschwinden
distance Ferne
double-handed doppeltes Spiel
doubt Zweifel
draw ziehen
dreamer Träumer
drinks cupboard Hausbar
driving lesson Fahrstunde
driving test Führerscheinprüfung
duck Ente

earth Erde
easy leicht; einfach
economy Wirtschaft
embarrassed verlegen
embarrassment Verlegenheit
empty leer

enemy Feind
engine Maschine; Lokomotive
english englisch
enter betreten
entirely vollkommen
escape entfliehen
especially besonders
even so trotz allem
exact genau
excellent ausgezeichnet
exciting aufregend
excursion Ausflug
expectation Erwartung
experience Erfahrung
explain erklären
expression Ausdruck
eye Auge

face Gesicht
fact Tatsache
false teeth Gebiß
fantastic wunderbar
fashion in in Mode
fast (hold sth) festhalten
fault Fehler
feeling Gefühl
fence Zaun
flash blitzen
float schweben
flush spülen
follow folgen
forehead Stirn
foreigner Ausländer
forest Wald
forget to vergessen zu tun

forward nach vorne
friend Freund
frightening beängstigend
front of (in) vor
frown Stirn runzeln
funeral Begräbnis
furious wütend

gate Eingang
gaze Blick
get up aufstehen
girl Mädchen
glow leuchten
goddei Guten Tag (dänisch)
goods Waren; Güter
gratitude Dankbarkeit
grave (n) Grab
grin grinsen
ground Boden
gun Gewehr
guts Mut

hair Haar
half-circle Halbkreis
hammock Hängematte
hang hängen
hardly kaum
hate hassen
headhunter Kopfjäger
health certificate Gesundheitszeugnis
help Hilfe
hide sich verstecken
high speed hohe Geschwindigkeit

high tide Hochflut
hill Hügel
hitch-hike per Anhalter fahren
hoop Reifen
horizon Horizont
horror Schrecken
hum summen
human Menschen
hurry (n) Eile
hurry (v) eilen
hysterical hysterisch

idea Idee
illness Krankheit
imitate nachahmen
immigrant Einwanderer
immigration Einwanderung
impertinent unverschämt
impression Eindruck
in fact tatsächlich
in front of vor
indignant entrüstet
insult (n) Beleidigung
intelligent intelligent
intercom Bordsprechanlage
introduction Einführung
invisible unsichtbar
island Insel

jump (vor Freude) hüpfen

keep out Zutritt verboten
kick anstoßen
kneel knien
know how to wissen wie ...

land landen
landing strip Rollbahn
landscape Landschaft
language Sprache
last dauern
laugh (n) Lachen
laugh (v) lachen
leaf Blatt
lift Aufzug
light Licht
limit (n) Grenze
lock on zusammenschließen
loneliness Einsamkeit
look after aufpassen; versorgen
loyal treu
lucky glücklich
luggage Gepäck

main Haupt...
maintenance Wartung
map Karte
march off fortgehen
market town Marktflecken
master (n) Herr
matter (for tht) übrigens
meat Fleisch
military militärisch
minister Minister
miserable elend
miss verfehlen
missionary Missionar
mistake Fehler
mohammedan Mohammedaner
moon Mond
mostly meistens

mouth Mund
move bewegen; handeln
move off fortfahren
move up hochfahren
movement Bewegung
mumble murmeln
murder ermorden
mutter murmeln

necessary notwendig
Neece Eigenname e. Kekssorte
new neu
nod nicken
noise Geräusch; Lärm
nonsense Unsinn
nor noch
nothing nichts
notice (n) Bekanntmachung
notice (v) bemerken

observation room Beobachtungsraum
odd seltsam
officer Polizist
open öffnen
organise organisieren
out of sight außer Sichtweite
out of the question außer Frage
over (be) zu Ende
overtake überholen
oxygen Sauerstoff

package tour Gruppenreise
pale blaß
papers Papiere

parent Eltern(teil)
parson Pfarrer
part Teil
partner Partner
pass (n) Bergpaß
pastor Pfarrer
patient geduldig
peppermint tea Pfefferminztee
personal feature persönliche Merkmale
perspiration Schweiß
piece Stück
pile (n) Stapel
pinhead Stecknadelkopf
Plantlife Promotion Laboratory experimentelles Pflanzenlabor
plane (intell.) Ebene
plastic dome Plastikzelt
plate Teller
plot Verschwörung
plunge eintauchen
pocket Hosentasche
point at zeigen auf
points (n) Weichen
poison Gift
polite höflich
political politisch
pony Pony
porter Kofferträger
possible möglich
post Pfahl
power Maschinen; Macht
pray beten
prayer Gebets ...
prayer-rug Gebetsteppich

present (n) Geschenk
press drücken
priest Priester
programme Programm
proud stolz
psychology Psychologie
pull herausziehen; zupfen
pullover Pullover
purpose Zweck
purser Zahlmeister
put up with durchgehen lassen
pyrenees Pyrenäen

queue Schlange
quick schnell

raft Floß
rain regnen
rain forest Regenwald
raincoat Regenmantel
rainy season Regenzeit
reach erreichen
ready bereit
reasonable vernünftig
reception Empfang (Rezeption)
recognize erkennen
recycle wieder brauchbar machen
refuse weigern; ablehnen
register bestellen
regretful voller Bedauern
remember erinnern
reserved (adj) reserviert
respectable ehrwürdig

revenge sich rächen
rice Reis
risk (n) Risiko
roar brüllen
rock (v) holpern
rock Fels
rogue Gauner
roll (n) Rolle
room Platz
rope Seil
routine Routine
ruin (v) zugrunde richten
rule (n) Regel
rumour Gerücht

safe sicher
safety Sicherheit
Sandhurst Name einer militärischen Akademie
savage Wilder
save oneself sth einsparen
sea-bird Seevogel
seal Seehund
seated (stay) sitzen bleiben
seem scheinen
service Gottesdienst
set fire to in Brand setzen
set foot Fuß setzen
several einige; mehrere
shadow Schatten
she-goat Ziege (weibl.)
shelf Regal
ship (space-) Raumschiff
shipwreck Schiffswrack
shoot down abschießen

shore Strand
shoulder Schulter
shrug Achselzucken
shuttle (n) Raumfähre
sick (be) krank sein
sick (feel) sich krank fühlen
side Seite
sign (n) Zeichen; Schild
silence Stille
silly dumm
similarity Ähnlichkeit
sink (n) Waschbecken
sit sitzen
sit down sich hinsetzen
situation Situation
skin Haut
sky Himmel
sleep schlafen
sleeping quarter Schlafkabine
sleeve Ärmel
small klein
smell (n) Geruch
smuggler Schmuggler
smuggling business Schmuggelgeschäfte
society Gesellschaft
sofa Sofa
soft weich
son Sohn
sound klingen
space Weltraum
space suit Raumanzug
spaceship comp Raumschiffgesellschaft
spar Tragholm

special Sonder ...
Spindizzy Name für ein Raumschiff, das eigene Schwerkraft produziert
spoil verderben
stand up aufstehen
star Stern
startle jem. erschrecken
starve verhungern
station-master Bahnhofsvorsteher
steward Steward
stolen gestohlen
stomach Magen
strength Kraft
strict streng
strong stark
studies (n) Studium
study (v) studieren
suddenly plötzlich
suitcase Koffer
suppose annehmen
sway and dip auf und abdümpeln
swing schaukeln
swing open auffliegen

take notice sich kümmern um
take off starten
taste (good) (guter) Geschmack
tear Träne
tender zärtlich
tent Zelt
terrible schrecklich
therefore deshalb

thick dick
thin schmal
though obwohl
thought Gedanke
ticket Karte
tidy nett
tie down festbinden
timber pile Holzhaufen
touch berühren
tour of duty Dienstreise
towards in Richtung auf
track of (lose) Spur verlieren
trade certificate Handelsgenehmigung
tramp Vagabund
trap Falle
travel agent Reiseberater
traveller Reisender
tremble zittern
trouble (take) sich die Mühe machen
trustworthy vertrauenswürdig
tunnel Tunnelgang
turn wenden
turn on anstellen
turn round sich umdrehen

unattached ledig
understand verstehen
uninhibited frei
unkind unfreundlich
unlucky Pech (haben)
up north vom Norden
upright aufgerichtet
upset zum Kentern bringen

use (n) Gebrauch
usual gewöhnlich

valley Tal
vicar Vikar
village Dorf

wait warten
wander gehen; wandern
watch Armbanduhr

wave winken
weapon Waffe
wear tragen
whip peitschen
whistle pfeifen
wink zwinkern
wonder sich fragen
wood Wald
word Wort
wrinkle (n) Falte

Acknowledgements

Der Verlag dankt den folgenden Personen, Firmen und Institutionen für die Überlassung von Copyright-Material:

BUSINESS TRAVELLER, for A Most Unusual Journey